How Long Dog's Tail?

Jill Bever and Sheilah Currie

This is my dog, Puff.

I'm going to use crayons

to measure his tail.

I think I'll need two crayons.

2

My dog's name is Lulu.

I'll measure her tail, too.

I think her tail is

five crayons long.

Puff's tail is very short.

It's only one crayon long.

Lulu's tail is longer.

It is five crayons long.

I used a ribbon to measure

around my dog, Jack.

I think I'll need five bones to

measure the ribbon.

My dog, Goldy, is bigger.

I think I'll need about ten bones

to measure the ribbon that went

around her.

I was right. Jack is small.

I needed only five bones

to measure around him.

I needed more. Goldy is
very big. I needed eleven
bones to measure
around her.

Here is my dog, Woody.

How wide is he?

I think he is about

twelve cubes wide.

10

This is Minny.

She is a puppy.

I think she is

only five cubes wide.

Look! Woody is a big dog.

I needed fifteen cubes!

Minny is smaller.

She is only four cubes wide.

Here are all the dogs,

from tallest to shortest.

How many blocks high

is each dog?

Some of the dogs are big,

and some are small ...

but they **all** like treats!